THE
MULE DEER

BY
MARK E. AHLSTROM

EDITED BY
DR. HOWARD SCHROEDER
**Professor in Reading and Language Arts
Dept. of Elementary Education
Mankato State University**

PRODUCED AND DESIGNED BY
BAKER STREET PRODUCTIONS
Mankato, MN

CRESTWOOD HOUSE
Mankato, Minnesota

CIP

LIBRARY OF CONGRESS CATALOGING IN PUBLICATION DATA

Ahlstrom, Mark E.
  The mule deer.

  (Wildlife, habits & habitat)
  "Baker Street Productions."
  SUMMARY: An introduction to the mule deer, native of North America,
discussing its physical characteristics, habitats, and behavior.
  1. Mule deer--Juvenile literature. (1. Mule deer. 2. Deer.) I. Schroeder,
Howard. II. Baker Street Productions. III. Title. IV. Series.
QL737.U55A357   1987   599.73'57   87-614
ISBN 0-89686-324-7

International Standard
Book Number:
Library Binding 0-89686-324-7

Library of Congress
Catalog Card Number:
87-614

ILLUSTRATION CREDITS:

Cover Photo: Leonard Lee Rue III/Tom Stack & Associates
Leonard Lee Rue III/Tom Stack & Associates: 5
Mark E. Ahlstrom: 6, 8, 18, 43
John Shaw/Tom Stack & Associates: 11
Milton Rand/Tom Stack & Associates: 12
Lynn M. Stone: 14, 17, 23, 39
Brian Parker/Tom Stack & Associates: 20
Phil & Loretta Hermann: 24-25
Gary R. Zahm/DRK Photo: 27, 31
Nancy Adams/Tom Stack & Associates: 28, 40-41
Marty Cordano/DRK Photo: 33
Jeff Foott/Tom Stack & Associates: 35
Larry R. Ditto/Tom Stack & Associates: 37

CRESTWOOD HOUSE
Hwy. 66 South, Box 3427
Mankato, MN 56002-3427

TABLE OF CONTENTS

INTRODUCTION:

Mule deer everywhere

In 1970, a group of us decided to go "out West" to hunt mule deer for the first time. We were all from Minnesota, and had never hunted for any deer except whitetails. Like many hunters, we had dreamed for many years about making a trip to the mountains of the western U.S. or Canada.

Also, like many hunters, we did not know very much about mule deer. The one thing we thought we knew was that mule deer lived in the mountains. In other words, if we wanted to hunt for these deer of the West, we had to go into the high country. That fact, of course, only added to our excitement. This was going to be "big-time" hunting!

The mountains closest to Minnesota are found in the Black Hills National Forest of western South Dakota. After some checking, we were pleased to learn there were a good number of mule deer in the Black Hills. So we were all set. A trip of about five hundred miles (800 k) would put us in the high country.

After months of talk and planning, we finally left our Minnesota homes in the middle of a November night. We were not quite halfway across South Dakota when

Mule deer are found only in western North America.

the sky began to lighten in the East. As we crossed the Missouri River and began to drive up through the "breaks" of the west side of the valley, the sun popped over the horizon.

The slanting sunlight made the frost on the ground sparkle like diamonds! What a sight! This little "light show" almost caused us to miss the small herd of deer on a distant hillside.

"Hey, what are those?" someone asked. "They look like mule deer, but there aren't supposed to be any mule deer here."

A small herd of mule deer feeds at sunrise in the Missouri River "breaks" of South Dakota.

We stopped the car and got out the binoculars. There was no doubt about it. We had all looked at enough outdoor magazines to recognize the large Mickey-Mouse ears of the deer that stood staring at us. They **were** mule deer.

And those weren't the only mule deer we saw during the first hour of daylight on the west side of the Missouri River. Whenever there were gullies and draws to break up the grasslands, we saw small bunches of "mulies." We were all scratching our heads, wondering why we **had** to go to the mountains to find mule deer. This didn't make sense!

We drove on because our license only allowed us to hunt in the Black Hills. Once in the Black Hills, we learned something else. Most of the mule deer weren't in the mountains. Instead, they seemed to prefer the foothills that led up into the mountains.

The big-eared deer surprised us once more on the way home. We were getting bored with the interstate highway, so we decided to take a little side trip. The two-lane road took us through the Badlands National Monument. It was nearing sunset as we drove through this wonder of nature.

Anyone who has been to the Badlands knows that they are as close as you can get to being a desert—without really being a desert. Very little of anything grows, except in the lowest areas. And that's where we saw the mule deer. The animals were feeding wherever a little water allowed grasses and other plants to grow.

Some mule deer live in the "badlands" of the west. These deer were photographed at sunset in the Badlands National Monument.

In the space of one week we had seen mule deer on the prairie hillsides west of the Missouri River. We had seen them in both the foothills and the mountains of the Black Hills. Finally, we had seen them in the desert-like habitat of the Badlands. In short, mule deer didn't just live in the mountains. They seemed to be everywhere!

I, for one, quickly realized that I had a lot to learn about the mule deer. I knew quite a bit about the whitetail deer, but almost nothing about the "other deer" of western North America. I'd like to now share some of what I learned.

—M.E.A.

CHAPTER ONE:

Part of a large family

There are about fifty species, or kinds, of mammals that make up the deer family. Members of this family, known as *Cervidae,* are found on every continent, except Antarctica. The North American members include the moose, elk, caribou, whitetail, and mule deer.

Biologists think that ancestors of these five species of deer migrated to North America across the Bering Land Bridge. These early deer, along with many other animals, followed a narrow strip of land that once joined Russia and Alaska. The animals fanned out across North America before glaciers covered much of the continent.

By studying fossils, experts say that whitetail deer and mule deer evolved from a common ancestor. The whitetail *(Odocoileus virginianus)* developed because of its habitat in the hardwood forests of the East. The mule deer *(Odocoileus hemionus)* evolved in the dry, rugged badlands and mountains of the West. These two species, which we commonly know as deer, are found only in North America. Moose, elk, and caribou are found elsewhere in the world.

At present, biologists say there are seven subspecies, or types, of mule deer. They are the Rocky Mountain mule deer, California mule deer, southern mule deer, Peninsula mule deer, desert mule deer, Columbian blacktail, and Sitka blacktail.

You might notice something strange about this list of deer. Five of the types are called mule deer, while two of them are called blacktail deer. There is a reason for this—the experts have been arguing about how to classify the Columbian and Sitka blacktails.

Until recently, it was thought that there were enough differences between the two groups to make the blacktails a separate species. And, in fact, they were classified as such. Recent studies, however, seem to show that the groups are not different enough to be thought of as two separate species. However, because there are **some** basic differences, the experts think it is proper to keep the distinct common names. In this book, they will be talked about separately, as either blacktails or mule deer.

A large range

There are somewhere between six and seven million blacktails and mule deer living in North America. About one-and-a-half million are blacktail subspecies. A little over five million are mule deer subspecies. This compares to about twelve million whitetails of all types.

Mule deer live in the mountains, plains, deserts, and near the coast of western North America. Blacktails live only along the coast between central California and Alaska. (Refer to the map on page 45.)

The Rocky Mountain mule deer has the largest range of any member of the deer family in North America. It is also the biggest mule deer. Its range extends north to the Northwest Territories, east to the Dakotas and Nebraska, south to the middle of New Mexico and Arizona, and west nearly to the Pacific Ocean. There are even reports of this mule deer in Minnesota and Iowa!

Rocky Mountain mule deer are the largest subspecies of mule deer. Bucks, or males, often weigh over two hundred pounds (91 kg).

The California mule deer, as its name implies, is found only in California. It inhabits the southern half of the state from the Sierra Mountains to the Pacific Ocean. It shares the northern parts of its range with the Columbian blacktail. Rocky Mountain mule deer share parts of its range to the east.

The southern mule deer is found in extreme southern California and the northern part of the Baja Peninsula. The Peninsula mule deer is found only in the southern two-thirds of Baja. Like the California mule deer, these last two are smaller than the Rocky Mountain type.

The desert mule deer has a range that is second only

Desert mule deer usually have the largest ears. Experts think that the extra blood vessels in their ears allows more body heat to escape, helping the deer stay cool.

to the Rocky Mountain mule deer. Its range extends from southern Arizona, New Mexico, and Texas into the middle of Mexico. This subspecies can sometimes be as large as Rocky Mountain mule deer. But because its forage is often in short supply, it almost never gets as heavy as its northern cousin.

The Columbian blacktail's range extends along the Pacific coast from the middle of California to the middle of British Columbia. To the east, its range often overlaps with the Rocky Mountain mule deer.

The original range of the Sitka blacktail extended from the Queen Charlotte Islands north through the islands and mainland of the Alaska Panhandle. Transplants in the early 1900's extended their range to areas around Yakutat and Prince William Sound. Later, transplants were also made to Afognak and Kodiak Islands.

Both types of blacktails are usually smaller than any of their mule deer cousins. The Sitka blacktail is the smallest of the mule deer species.

A varied habitat

No other big-game animal survives in such a wide variety of habitats as the mule deer. Their home ranges vary from the thick forests on the top of mountains, to dry, treeless deserts. The habitats of the blacktails are almost as varied. Blacktails live on the tundra of Alaska, in the rain forests of the Pacific coast, and in the mountains and chaparral of northern California.

Both subspecies of blacktail deer live along the western coast of North America. Note the black tail!

There are a couple of things that most members of the mule deer species have in common. All subspecies are usually found on slopes—almost all of their habitat is either mountainous or hilly. The exceptions are a few mule deer who have found a home on the plains, and a few blacktails that survive on the tundra of Alaska. The other thing that they have in common is their inability to live near people. Unlike the whitetail, which has almost made a habit of living around people, mule deer and blacktail populations usually decline when people live nearby. Most mule deer and blacktails tend to live on slopes away from people.

The habitats of the five mule deer subspecies will often have one other thing in common. They usually contain far more open country than the habitats of either blacktails or whitetails. This is because most mule deer have learned to depend on their vision to warn them of danger at a distance.

Most blacktails, on the other hand, have come to rely on a dense, forest habitat for safety. Like most whitetails, they like to hide from their enemies. They rely on their ears and noses to warn them of danger.

Habitat types

Biologists divide mule deer habitat into three different types: mountain-foothill, prairie, and semidesert-shrub.

Because mountain-foothill habitats cover such a wide area of western North America, no two are exactly alike. Generally, mule deer in this type of habitat spend the summer months in the higher elevations in open forests. They spend the winter months on south-facing slopes of the foothills where snow is less likely to cover the shrubs that provide their food.

Prairies, with their rolling grasslands, provide little habitat for mule deer. Instead, it is the rough ''breaks'' along rivers, gullies in ''badlands,'' or brushy draws found throughout the prairies that attract mule deer. The deer spend summer and winter in the same general areas.

There are two kinds of semidesert-shrub habitat. One kind, found in Arizona, New Mexico, Texas, and Mexico has mostly creosote bush, mesquite, greasewood, chaparral, and cactus. The other kind, found in parts of Nevada, Utah, and Oregon contains sagebrush, saltbush, and winterfat. Small parts of these areas may also contain juniper, pinyon, or sparce pine forests at higher elevations. As might be expected, deer do not migrate from area to area in this habitat either.

Blacktails live in two types of habitat: coastal rain forest and woodland-chaparral.

The coastal rain forest habitat is found along the Pacific Coast from Northern California to southeastern Alaska. These coniferous, or evergreen, forests of redwood, fir, spruce, and cedar, feature a cool climate. There are many cloudy days, with a lot of rain throughout the year. The forests are thick and lush.

The woodland-chaparral habitats are of two types. The woodlands have oak and pine trees, with many shrubs and grassy openings. The chaparral types feature numerous shrubs, like manzanita and chamise. Periodic fires are very important in chaparral. Without fires, the shrubs become too dense for the deer to use. Fires often are set on purpose to ensure that the deer will have what they need. Woodland-chaparral habitat is found along the central coast ranges in California.

Both mule deer and blacktails seem to adapt rather easily to a change of habitat. Blacktails have been transplanted from rain forests to the arid chaparrals of

This Columbian blacktail fawn wanders through a grassy opening in its rain-forest habitat.

Where their ranges overlap, whitetail and mule deer often live close to each other. In this area of South Dakota, whitetails live in the brushy area near the river, while mule deer live in the hills.

California, and even the tundra of Alaska. Mule deer have been moved from the mountains to desert areas with success. It seems amazing that mule deer and blacktails, which are unable to live near people, are able to handle being transplanted so well.

By comparison, transplants of whitetails, which often live near people, often end in disaster. Experts think that whitetails are simply too nervous to handle the stress of being moved. Perhaps the fact that mule deer and blacktails are naturally more calm allows them to adapt more easily to new areas.

CHAPTER TWO:

How mule deer and blacktails got their names

Both the whitetail species and the mule deer species belong to the same genus, or subdivision, of the deer family. Thus, they have the same genus name, *Odocoileus,* which is a rough translation of the Greek word for hollow or concave tooth. This name was given because the man who named the first deer in North America found a fossil of a deer's tooth. He added the species name, *virginianus,* because the tooth was found in Virginia. This deer later became known as the whitetail.

Because the whitetail was the first deer to be discovered, it became what biologists call the "type species." All different species discovered later would carry the same genus name. That's what happened to the mule deer. The same man, while on a trip to what is now South Dakota, was the first biologist to see a mule deer. He must have been impressed by the animal's large ears. The species name for both mule deer and blacktails, *hemionus,* is the Greek word that means mule or part-donkey. The mule, of course, also has very large ears.

Mule deer were named for their large, mule-like ears.

The blacktails' official Latin names have nothing to do with how the animals look. Their common name, blacktail, refers to the fact that the tops of their tails are mostly black. In contrast, both mule deer and white-tails have quite a bit of white hair that shows on their tails.

Those amazing antlers!

When most people think of deer, the first thing to come to their minds is antlers. No deer grows larger antlers than the Rocky Mountain mule deer. The antlers of other subspecies of mule deer and blacktails, while not as large, are just as majestic.

It is important to know that horns and antlers are not the same thing. Horns are made of keratin, as are hoofs and fingernails. They are never shed, but grow larger each year. Wild sheep, bison, and cattle, for example, have horns. Antlers, on the other hand, are true bone. Unlike most bones, however, they are solid and have no marrow. Antlers are shed every year and a new set is grown.

All but two members of the *Cervidae* family grow antlers. The only antlered species whose females **normally** grow antlers are caribou. Females of other members of the deer family, including mule deer and blacktails, have been known to grow antlers. But when they do, it is a "freak" event.

Only the bucks, or male mule deer and blacktails, normally grow antlers. Small knobs, called pedicels, will form on a buck's forehead when he is two to three months old. When he is about six months of age, the bumps are usually quite easy to see. At this stage the deer is known as a "button buck." Growth usually stops at this point, and resumes the following spring.

The next year, most bucks will grow either single "spikes" or "forked" antlers with two "points" on each side. If bucks have plenty of food, they almost always will grow forked antlers as yearlings. These first antlers are shed during the following winter.

The typical four-point adult antlers of mule deer and blacktail bucks are first formed at the beginning of their third year. These antlers branch equally above the base to form four major tines, or points, on each side. In contrast, the antlers of whitetails form several small tines rising from a single main beam on each side.

As long as their diet is good, most bucks will grow a larger set of antlers each year. Usually they just get thicker and longer. The world record mule deer antlers are truly huge. The right side at its longest point is over thirty inches (77 cm) long, and the left side is over twenty-eight inches (72 cm) long. The base of each antler is more than five inches (13 cm) around. The inside spread, or distance between the two antlers, is over thirty inches (77 cm). By way of comparison, the world record blacktail antlers are each about twenty-four inches (62 cm) long.

Antlers start growing each year in April or May. During the time they are growing, they are soft and are covered with a fuzzy skin, called "velvet." During the peak growth period of the summer, the antlers may grow three inches (7.7 cm) in a week! Growth is usually complete by September. Soon after, the velvet is shed, exposing the hard-as-bone antlers. Most antlers fall off in January or February, usually within a day or two of each other.

After bucks reach their seventh or eighth year, the antlers they grow start getting a bit smaller each year until the bucks die.

The antlers of this Columbian blacktail are covered with "velvet." They are in the process of growing, and are just starting to form the two main branches.

23

A mature Rocky Mountain mule deer is quite a sight!

The senses and coloration

Like most wild animals, mule deer and blacktails depend on the senses of smell, sight, and hearing for survival. Their large ears, especially the mule deer's, allow them to hear danger at a great distance. Their sense of smell also is very good, and probably is the sense they depend on most. It allows them to identify the scent of people or predators. Because they live in more open spaces, mule deer depend more on their eyesight then blacktails do. For mule deer, eyesight acts as a distant-early-warning system.

Just as important for survival is the ability to hide from danger. The colors of the deer's coat help them do that. Their basic color in the summer is reddish-brown. The hairs of this coat are solid and there is no undercoat. The winter coats are grayish-brown in color. This coat is made of hollow ''guard hairs'' that cover a soft, curly undercoat. This arrangement is much warmer than the summer coat. The colors of these seasonal coats help the deer to blend with their habitat. The dull winter coats blend with dull winter colors, while the darker summer coats blend with the richer colors of summer. The deer molt, or change, their coats in the spring and fall.

Nature also goes one step further to help these deer protect themselves. The deer that live in light-colored habitats, like desert mule deer, have lighter coats than

The coats of desert mule deer are usually lighter in color than other mule deer. This allows them to blend with their desert habitat.

the deer that live in the darker habitats of the mountains.

The patches of color on these deer help to break up its outline. The nose and a band around the muzzle are black. The face and the area around the eyes are white, while the top of the head is black. The large ears are rimmed with black and lined with white. There are two patches of white on the throat, which are separated by a patch of dark hair. The cheeks are gray. White hairs cover the belly and the inside of the legs. The hoofs are black.

The effect of all this coloring is to give the mule deer and the blacktail a "dappled" look. It's much like the effect of sunlight shining through the leaves of a tree onto the ground. The deer can be very hard to see, especially if they are lying down.

Tails tell a tale

It is important to know some things about the color of a deer's tail. For tails alone will allow you to know if you're looking at a whitetail, a mule deer, or a blacktail.

The whitetail has, by far, the largest tail—most are from eleven to thirteen inches (28-33 cm) long. When held erect the tails flare out to a width of ten to eleven inches (25-28 cm). The top of the tail is brown or almost black, with a border of white. The entire underside of the tail is white.

The tail of the blacktail usually is about nine inches (23 cm) long. The hairs on the top of the tail are brownish-black, and some of these dark hairs run all

Unlike the tail of a blacktail deer—which is mostly black, the mule deer's tail is only black at the tip.

the way to the tip. There often is a narrow white border along the sides of the bottom third of the tail. The underside of the tail is white, but it doesn't flare out like the whitetail's.

The mule deer's tail is unique, in that it is a bit narrower in the middle than at the end. The upper portion of the tail is brown, the middle is white, and the tip is black. Except for the tip, the underside of the tail is white. Like the blacktail's tail, the hairs cannot be flared.

One word of caution—if you see a tail that doesn't fit one of these descriptions, you are looking at a tail that belongs to a hybrid deer. Although it is rare, deer of different types do crossbreed, and their tails will be a mixture of their parents' tails.

Communication

Mule deer and blacktails, like whitetails, make use of scent glands, foot stamping, and vocal sounds to "talk" to one another. Of course, only the deer really know what is going on, but biologists have learned a few things about the deer's communications system.

All deer have four main scent glands: preorbital (in front of the eyes), interdigital (between the toes), tarsal (on the inside of the hocks), and metatarsal (on the outside of the back legs). There also is a fifth spot, which is a scent area on the forehead.

Recent studies seem to show that mule deer, especially large bucks, use the preorbital glands to mark their territory on overhanging branches. Large bucks spend a lot of time rubbing these glands on the branches. Small bucks and does (female deer) spend a lot of time sniffing where the bucks have rubbed. Blacktail bucks seem to use the scent area on their foreheads in the same way. This activity goes on all year long, but the experts aren't sure why the deer do it.

The interdigital glands between the two center toes (the hoofs) of each foot allow deer to track one another. Experts think that each deer has its own odor. This, for example, allows a doe to find a fawn (the newborn of all deer) that has wandered off on its own.

Biologists think that the tarsal gland may be the most important of all. They base this feeling on the fact that deer pay much attention to this gland. These glands, on the inside of the hocks on the rear legs, have tufts of hair on which deer constantly urinate. Whenever deer meet they smell each others hocks, and often lick them. The scent given off by the glands seems to be the main way that bucks and does keep track of each other during the rut, or mating season. This is important for mule deer and blacktails, for they don't make "scrapes" to keep track of each other like whitetails do during the rut.

No one seems to know why deer have metatarsal glands. Because these glands on the outside of the rear legs are so large, they must have a purpose. The glands may allow deer to deposit scent on the ground while

A mule deer doe follows a scent trail during the "rut," or breeding season.

lying down, or they might pick up vibrations from the ground to warn of danger.

The scent area on a deer's forehead also is not fully understood. Experts know that mule deer, and especially blacktails, spend a lot of time rubbing their foreheads on the same branches every day. It is not yet known why the deer do it.

When deer hear or see something they cannot identify, they walk slowly forward and stamp their front feet on the ground. This action always gets the attention of the rest of the herd. Experts aren't sure if the stamping is meant to warn other deer or to scare a predator into showing itself.

Deer also make a variety of sounds to communicate with one another. When alarmed, they make a whistling snort by blasting air through their nostrils. When this sound is made, any deer in the area is on alert. While at rest, deer often make low-pitched, blaating sounds. During the rut, bucks make rather loud grunts. If fawns are separated from their mothers, they may bleat. Deer that are scared or injured make sounds that range from barks to roars to hisses. Biologists are just starting to learn what the sounds mean.

Feeding and bedding

Like other members of the deer family, mule deer and blacktails are ruminants. The first section of their four-part stomach, the rumen, is used to store food. When a deer feeds, it chews the food only as much as is needed for it to be swallowed. The rumen will be full after the deer has eaten about ten pounds (4.5 kg).

After the deer has found a safe place to bed down, the food is brought back up to its mouth in chunks, called cuds. The food is then completely chewed. When the food is swallowed for the second time, it goes into the second section of the stomach. It then slowly works its way through the rest of the digestive system.

Ruminants are able to eat a large amount of food in a short time. This reduces the amount of time they have to spend in open areas, where their food is found and they are in danger from predators.

Mule deer and blacktails are always alert to danger while feeding in open areas.

Blacktails and mule deer usually feed twice a day—very early in the morning and just before sunset. During the hunting season, or whenever they are bothered by people, they may feed before it gets light in the morning and after dark in the evening. Before a storm they may extend their feeding periods. During a cold winter, they may spend most of the day feeding.

These deer forage, or feed, on a wide variety of browse and grasses. They seem to have a natural ability to choose forage that is highest in food value. Because the forage that is available changes with the seasons and the weather, what the deer eat from time to time also changes.

Whenever they are available, grasses are an important food for mule deer and blacktails. They will even paw through snow to get at grass in the winter, if the snow is not too deep. Mule deer usually have to switch to browse in the winter because of deep snow. (Preferred browse plants are listed in the habitat section.) Blacktails usually have grasses available the year around, because they live in milder climates. Both deer will eat ferns, berries, nuts, cactus fruit, and wildflowers when they find them. In fact, these deer will eat just about anything they come across! They have learned to take what they can get at the moment.

At night, mule deer and blacktails usually bed down in the open in the middle of their feeding area. But after feeding in the morning they move to cover. They prefer a shaded ridge where they have a good view of the land

After feeding, this mule deer has found a safe place to bed down and chew its "cud."

around them. A high position also allows the rising thermal air currents to carry the odors of danger up both sides of the ridge.

Except in times of severe drought, deer do not have much need for water. They get all the moisture they need from the food they eat. But you can bet that they know where every water hole in their area is located! The same is true for mineral "licks." These natural deposits of salt and other minerals draw deer like magnets, especially after a long, hard winter.

Equipped for its habitat

There is a rule of thumb in nature that the largest members of a species will live in areas with the coldest temperatures. The reason is simple. The larger the body, the less the surface area that is exposed relative to its weight. The result is a reduced loss of body heat.

The mule deer species, *O. hemionus,* is no exception. The Rocky Mountain mule deer must put up with the coldest winters, and it is the largest subspecies. Average adult males weigh 163 pounds (74 kg), are 60 inches (152 cm) long, and stand 38 inches (96 cm) tall at the shoulder. It's common for an old buck to weigh over 200 pounds (91 kg) and stand 42 inches (107 cm) tall at the shoulder. Females up to the age of three years will be about twenty percent smaller. After that time they stop growing, while the bucks get bigger. The largest known Rocky Mountain mule deer had a dressed weight of 380 pounds (172 kg), with an estimated live weight of 456 pounds (207 kg).

The Sitka blacktail is usually the smallest subspecies. However, the Columbian blacktail is not much larger. Average weights for four-year-old deer of both types are about 135 pounds (61 kg) for bucks and 90 pounds (41 kg) for does.

Another way in which nature has equipped mule deer and blacktails for their habitat is their strange, bounding gallop. While the whitetail has a graceful gallop, these deer gallop by pushing off from the ground with all four feet at once. It looks like they're using a pogo stick! However, this style of running is perfect for the

A mule deer gallops by pushing off the ground with all four feet at the same time. Jackrabbits run the same way.

steep, rocky terrain in which mule deer and blacktails live. If they have to, these deer can turn in any direction—or even turn completely around—in the course of a single bound. And though it may be hard to believe, mule deer and blacktails can run just as fast as a whitetail—thirty-five miles per hour (56 kph). They are also very good swimmers.

Enemies and diseases

In areas where mountain lions have not been exterminated, they are the main enemy of the mule deer. When possible, a lion will kill one or two deer a week. In the northern parts of the mule deer's range, wolves also prey on the deer. These large predators serve the purpose of controlling the size of a deer herd. In areas where the predators have been eliminated, the deer herds often get too large for the food supply. The result is a large die-off caused by starvation.

The main enemies of all blacktails are black bears and grizzly bears. Bald eagles and golden eagles sometimes kill fawns.

Hoof-and-mouth disease is the only disease known to have a serious effect on deer. Infected cattle can pass the disease to deer. More than twenty thousand California mule deer were once killed by the disease.

Wolves feed on a mule deer that they have killed.

The rut is carefully timed

The rut, or breeding season, occurs in the fall of the year for all deer. Biologists think that the shorter hours of daylight trigger the urge for deer to mate. The exact timing depends on the climate in which the deer live. This timing has evolved over the centuries to give the fawns the best chance for survival.

Most blacktails breed from September to November. After about a two hundred day gestation period, the fawns are born between May and July. This gives the fawns time to develop before very wet and cold weather arrives in the fall.

Two mule deer bucks fight for the right to breed the does during the rut. Usually the largest, strongest buck wins all the fights, and

Rocky Mountain mule deer do most of their breeding in November and December, and the fawns are born in late June and July. This allows the fawns to escape a late spring or an early fall snowstorm.

breeds most of the does in his home range.

Desert mule deer breed the latest of all, mainly during December and January. This allows the fawns to be born in July and August after the spring drought. It is important that these desert deer have plenty of forage so the does can produce milk.

Most mule deer and blacktail does give birth to one or two fawns. Sometimes as many as three or four are born. The fawns weigh from five to seven pounds (2.3-3.2 kg) at birth, and their reddish coats are covered with white spots. Within a very short time, the fawns are on their feet and walking. Almost immediately, the doe leads them away and hides them in tall grass or plants. The doe stays away from her fawns except to nurse them every three or four hours. This is so her scent will not attract predators to the fawns. The fawns themselves are born with almost no odor.

Within two weeks, fawns are strong enough to follow their mothers. By fall, when they quit nursing, most fawns will weigh about eighty pounds (36 kg). Fawns stay with their mothers until their mothers give birth again the next spring. Sometimes a doe will allow her yearlings to rejoin her after she has given birth. Young females may stay with her for two years, while males usually leave after one year.

Most does breed for the first time when they are one-and-a-half years old. However, because the largest bucks don't allow young bucks near does during the breeding season, a buck may be three-and-a-half before he breeds for the first time.

If they are not killed by accident, or hunting, mule deer and blacktails live for about ten years. The oldest known blacktail was a doe that lived to "a ripe old age" of twenty-two.

Seasonal migration

With the coming of winter, any mule deer that live in the mountains move down to sheltered valleys. They need to move where the snow is not so deep. Most mule deer have to go only a short distance to reach their winter range. Some, however, have to go much further! One herd, known as the Interstate deer herd, travels

Most Rocky Mountain mule deer spend the winter in protected foothill areas like this where snow doesn't cover their food.

about one hundred miles from its summer range in Oregon to its winter range in California. Of course, the herd also has to make the return trip in the spring. The Tehoma herd travels about the same distance within the state of California.

Because blacktails don't have to contend with much snow, they usually live on the same range during winter and summer. The same is true for desert mule deer and others in the southern part of the mule deer range.

The future is not clear

No one can say for sure what the future holds for mule deer and blacktails. There are still many things that the experts have to learn about these deer. For example, no one really knows why the herds suddenly increased during the late 1960's and early 1970's. Nor does anyone know why their numbers suddenly went down in the late 1970's.

While we're waiting for the answers, probably the best thing we can do is to avoid making any quick decisions. We've got to learn what the effects of land development really are on the herds. We've also got to take a close look at how to best regulate hunting for the long-range good of the deer.

Only then will we be able to say that there are "mule deer everywhere," well into the future.

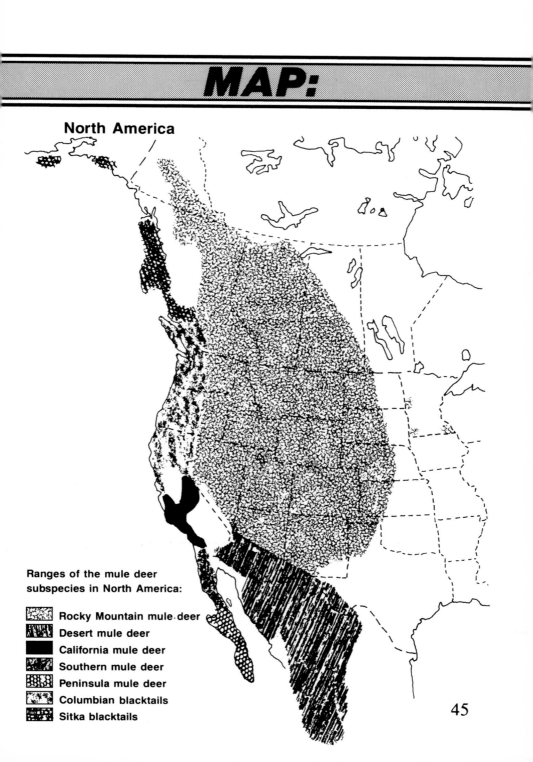

MAP:

North America

Ranges of the mule deer
subspecies in North America:

- Rocky Mountain mule deer
- Desert mule deer
- California mule deer
- Southern mule deer
- Peninsula mule deer
- Columbian blacktails
- Sitka blacktails

45

INDEX/GLOSSARY:

WILDLIFE
HABITS & HABITAT

READ AND ENJOY THE SERIES:

If you would like to know more about all kinds of wildlife, you should take a look at the other books in this series.

You'll find books on bald eagles and other birds. Books on alligators and other reptiles. There are books about deer and other big-game animals. And there are books about sharks and other creatures that live in the ocean.

In all of the books you will learn that life in the wild is not easy. But you will also learn what people can do to help wildlife survive. So read on!